THE EARTH
and Its Neighbors

by Donna Latham

PEARSON
Scott
Foresman

DK

Galileo was the first scientist to study the planets with a telescope.

Into Orbit

In 1610, a scientist named Galileo first discovered Saturn's rings. He had built his own small telescope and became the first person to use one to observe the nighttime sky. Galileo didn't know what the rings were. His telescope was too weak to make them out clearly.

Through his observations of the Moon, he announced that its surface was pitted. Others had claimed that it was smooth. Galileo also discovered the four largest moons of the planet Jupiter.

Now, centuries later, we know a lot more about the Sun, Moon, and planets than Galileo did. Scientists have discovered that there are nine planets traveling around the Sun. They have taken close-up pictures of these planets and mapped their paths around the Sun. We have even sent people to walk on the Moon! What other discoveries have we made about the objects that are our neighbors in space? Let's find out!

How does Earth move?

The Orbit of Earth

You can't feel it, but right now, Earth is traveling through space. It's one of nine ball-shaped planets circling the Sun. Vital to our lives, the Sun is a star at the center of our solar system. The solar system is made up of the Sun, nine planets, and other objects that revolve around it.

Each of the planets travels around the Sun in its own path, at its own pace. An orbit is the path that a planet follows around the Sun. The planets share the same type of orbit. Each has an elliptical orbit. That means the orbit is shaped like an oval.

The planets don't travel around the Sun alone. They take their own orbiting moons with them. Many other smaller objects travel around the Sun too.

Earth takes one year to complete a revolution around the Sun. The Moon takes about twenty-eight days, or a month, to revolve around Earth.

Sun

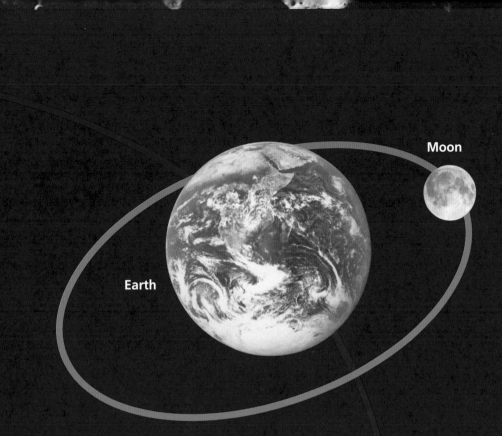

Moon

Earth

You know that a year on Earth is about 365 days, or twelve months, long. That's the time it takes Earth to travel around the Sun. Earth's orbit is huge, so it takes a long time for Earth to get all the way around it. A revolution is one complete orbit. So Earth's revolution around the Sun takes a year.

What causes Earth and the other planets to orbit the Sun? It's the pull of gravity between the Sun and the planets. Gravity is a force that draws objects together, and larger objects have more gravity than small ones. The Sun is massive, so the pull of its gravity is very strong. In fact, the pull of the Sun's gravity is so strong that it controls the orbits of all nine planets, even though they are millions and millions of miles away.

Night and Day

What causes the change between day and night? It happens because as Earth travels around the Sun, it also spins like a top. As the planet spins, only part of it faces the Sun at a time. It is day on this part of Earth. As the planet spins and this part is turned away from the Sun, it becomes night.

Earth always spins in the same direction, around an imaginary line called an **axis.** This line runs right through the center of Earth. Earth's axis tilts sideways a bit, just as a top's sometimes does.

As the top spins on its axis, it tilts, or slants to the side.

Rise and shine! During your twenty-four-hour day, you probably experience some hours of daylight and some of darkness.

One Day on Earth

A rotation is one whole spin of an object on its axis. It takes the Earth twenty-four hours to complete one rotation, so a day is twenty-four hours long. Earth's tilt causes the length of day and night to change. It changes all year long. Places closer to the poles experience more of a change than places near the equator.

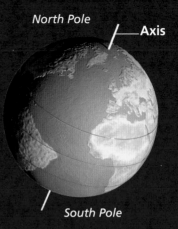

North Pole

Axis

South Pole

During some parts of the year, the Sun shines twenty-four hours a day at one pole, while the other has twenty-four hours of darkness.

The Temperature on Earth

When the Sun sets at night, temperatures drop. Since Earth spins swiftly on its axis, day follows night fairly quickly. So temperatures are mild enough for all life to exist. If the Earth spun more slowly, the long days would get very hot, and the long nights would get very cold.

Unlike some planets, Earth has a thick atmosphere. This blanket of air keeps Earth from getting too hot in the Sun's rays. It holds warmth near the Earth's surface. Some planets have no atmosphere. Their temperatures are too extreme for life. For example, the temperature on the sunny side of the Moon reaches hundreds of degrees, while the dark side is colder than any place on Earth.

The Pattern of the Seasons

Do you live in a place where there are four separate seasons? In some places, you might bundle up in a heavy coat during the winter, but wear shorts and flip-flops during the summer. What causes this pattern of changing temperatures?

As Earth moves around the Sun on its tilted axis, the tilt never changes. This means that sometimes the North Pole is tilted toward the Sun, and at other times the South Pole is. This makes the number of daylight hours change through the seasons, with more in the summer and fewer in the winter. It also changes the angle at which the Sun's rays hit Earth. Places that are tilted toward the Sun get more concentrated rays, which make temperatures warmer. Places tilted away from the Sun get more spread-out rays, which don't raise temperatures as much.

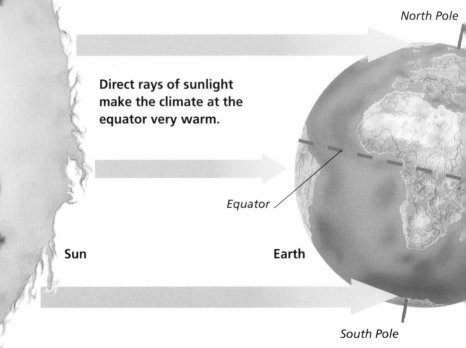

North Pole

Direct rays of sunlight make the climate at the equator very warm.

Equator

Sun

Earth

South Pole

Seasons on Earth

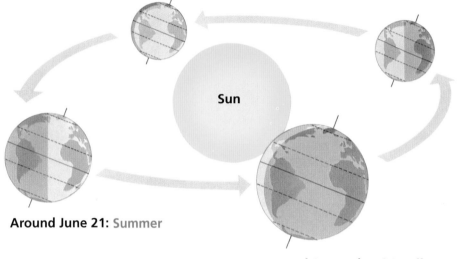

Around March 21: Spring

Around December 21: Winter

Sun

Around June 21: Summer

Around September 21: Fall

As Earth travels in its elliptical orbit, its distance from the Sun changes. You might think that this has something to do with the change in seasons, but it does not. Actually, Earth is closest to the Sun in January, when the Northern Hemisphere experiences winter. Earth's tilt is the real cause of the changing seasons.

This diagram shows the seasons in the northern half of the world. The southern half has the opposite seasons. For example, in June, July, and August, when it is summer in the United States, it is winter in Australia. Find the axis in each image of Earth. Notice that each is exactly the same.

The Solar System
The Paths That Planets Follow

A **satellite** is an object in orbit around another object. As you know, our solar system is made up of the Sun and its satellites. All the planets are huge. They are extremely far away from one another, so scientists measure their distances in astronomical units, or AUs. One AU equals the distance from Earth to the Sun, about 150 million kilometers.

The four planets closest to the Sun are Mercury, Venus, Earth, and Mars. They are made up mostly of rock and iron. Some of these planets have gases around them.

Saturn

Mars

Venus

Sun

Mercury

Earth

Farthest from the Sun are Jupiter, Saturn, Uranus, Neptune, and Pluto. Jupiter is the largest planet in the solar system, and Pluto is the smallest. Except for Pluto, these planets are all gas giants. Gas giants are huge planets that are made up of layers of gas. A gas giant does not have a solid surface as Earth does. Scientists think that they may have solid cores. As you can see, gas giants are much larger than Earth. All of the gas giants have rings. Most of the rings are very faint and cannot be seen in this illustration.

Did you know that planets do not give off their own light? When we see them in the sky, it is because of the light they reflect from the Sun.

The length of a year is different on each planet. The farther away from the Sun, the greater the time a planet takes to complete an orbit. So planets farther from the Sun have longer years.

Pluto

Jupiter

Uranus

Neptune

Time taken to orbit the Sun

Planet	Year
Mercury	88 Earth days
Venus	225 Earth days
Earth	365.26 Earth days (1 Earth year)
Mars	687 Earth days
Jupiter	12 Earth years
Saturn	29.5 Earth years
Uranus	84 Earth years
Neptune	164.5 Earth years
Pluto	248.5 Earth years

Planet Fact File

Let's compare the planets. Some are solid and rocky, and others are huge balls of gas. Below is a fact file of the planets, starting with Mercury, which is the planet closest to the Sun.

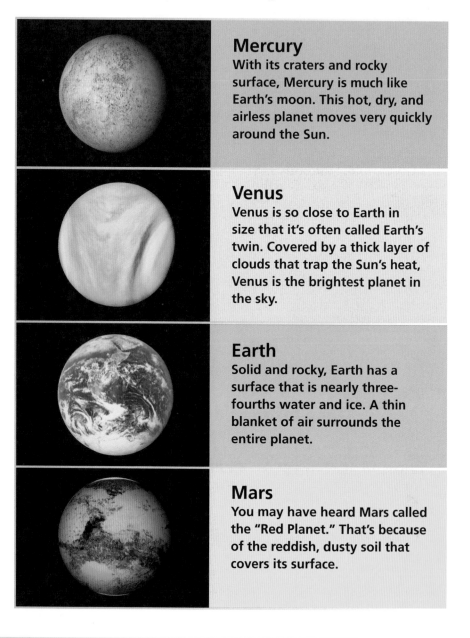

Mercury
With its craters and rocky surface, Mercury is much like Earth's moon. This hot, dry, and airless planet moves very quickly around the Sun.

Venus
Venus is so close to Earth in size that it's often called Earth's twin. Covered by a thick layer of clouds that trap the Sun's heat, Venus is the brightest planet in the sky.

Earth
Solid and rocky, Earth has a surface that is nearly three-fourths water and ice. A thin blanket of air surrounds the entire planet.

Mars
You may have heard Mars called the "Red Planet." That's because of the reddish, dusty soil that covers its surface.

Jupiter

The largest planet, Jupiter is a huge ball of gas and liquid. Scientists think Jupiter may also have a rocky core. Jupiter has faint rings.

Saturn

Saturn is a gas planet that is best known for its rings. Although all gas planets have rings made of dust, chunks of rock, and ice, Saturn has the most.

Uranus

Methane gas creates the blue-green color of this planet. Its winds give it bands of clouds. Uranus also has rings. The rings are not as bright as Saturn's.

Neptune

Neptune's atmosphere has huge storms. They look like dark spots when viewed through a telescope. Neptune also has rings. They are not easy to see.

Pluto

Pluto is the smallest and coldest planet in the solar system. It is usually the farthest planet from the Sun, but for part of its orbit it comes closer to the Sun than Neptune.

Visiting the Planets

If you could visit any planet in the solar system, which one would you choose? Although people may not be able to travel to all the planets, **space probes** have allowed us to explore them. Space probes are spacecraft that gather data without any people on board. They are equipped with special instruments and cameras. Since the 1970s, the United States has sent space probes to collect data from the planets. Here are some observations the probes have made.

Mercury

In 2004, two rovers, *Spirit* and *Opportunity*, landed on two separate areas of Mars.

Mariner 10 **first photographed Mercury in 1974.**

Opportunity

Venus has a thick layer of poisonous gases that make it impossible for you to breathe there.

Voyager 2

In 1986, *Voyager 2* visited Uranus, and in 1989 it visited Neptune. Through photos it sent back to Earth, we have discovered rings around all the gas giants, as well as several new moons. In addition, strong lightning storms were discovered on Jupiter.

The many spacecraft that have visited Mars have helped us learn that it has polar ice caps made of frozen water and frozen carbon dioxide. They have also sent back information about Mars' huge volcanoes.

Uranus

Mars

Comets and Asteroids

Only the largest comets can be seen without a telescope. Notice the comet's fuzzy tail.

Comets

Planets are not the only things orbiting the Sun! Comets orbit it too. A comet is a frozen mass of different types of ice and dust. The hard center of a comet is called the nucleus. Around the nucleus is a coma, or giant cloud of dust and gases. A comet may also have one or more tails. Tails and comas form only when the comet gets close to the Sun. There, the Sun melts the nucleus, which turns into gas. Then the comet gets the fuzzy look that we often associate with it.

Much smaller than planets, most comets come from areas beyond Pluto. You know that Pluto is the planet farthest from the Sun in our solar system, so comets travel a long distance. They travel in very stretched out, elliptical paths. Most comets are too small to be seen without a telescope.

Asteroids and Meteoroids

Asteroids also revolve around the Sun. An asteroid is a rocky mass that can range from the size of a tiny pebble to a width of several hundred kilometers. Some large asteroids even have smaller asteroids orbiting them.

Most asteroids in our solar system travel in a belt between Mars and Jupiter. Asteroids sometimes hit the inner planets, but this is very rare. Jupiter's powerful gravity usually holds asteroids in the asteroid belt.

Many asteroids have unusual shapes. Some look like potatoes, noses, and even dogs.

A meteoroid is a small asteroid. A meteor is a meteoroid that hits Earth's atmosphere. Meteors usually burn up in the atmosphere, but sometimes they make it through to strike the ground. These are called meteorites. One hit this site in Arizona thousands of years ago. The crater, or large, bowl-shaped hole, is 1,275 meters wide and 175 meters deep. Have you ever heard of a meteor shower? They happen when Earth passes through the orbit of a comet.

Arizona's Meteor Crater

What do we know about the Moon?

Like Earth and the planets, the Moon is ball-shaped.

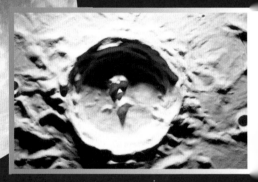

Many rocks or comets from space have struck the Moon, leaving pits called craters.

Moving with Earth

At about 384,000 km away, the Moon is Earth's closest neighbor in the solar system. The Moon is Earth's only natural satellite. It is about one-fourth the size of Earth, and it has no air or water. The Moon does have some ice, which may have come from comets crashing into it.

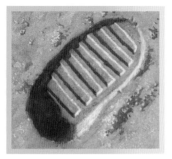

Footprint left behind by Neil Armstrong

Did you know that the Moon is the only place in the solar system, other than Earth, on which people have stood? On July 20, 1969, Neil Armstrong became the first person to actually set foot on the Moon. Because there is no air on the Moon to blow it away, his footprint is still there.

As the Moon orbits Earth, we can see only one side. This is called the "near side." This same side faces Earth at all times because of the Moon's rotation. Only astronauts have seen the other side of the Moon, called the "far side" or "dark side."

Some people once believed there was a man in the Moon. Without the telescopes we now use, they could only see the Moon with their eyes. Shadows and craters made it seem as if a "face" was looking back at them!

Using only your eyes, you can see some of the features of the Moon's surface. But with a telescope, you can see even more!

People of the past tried to explain why the Moon looks different over the course of a month. Today, we understand that **Moon phases,** or different shapes the Moon seems to have, are caused by the Sun. The Moon, Earth, and other bodies in the solar system get light only on the sides that face the Sun. The lighted side of the Moon doesn't always face us, so at different times of the month we see different amounts of its lit surface. When we see the entire lit side, we call it a full moon. When the lit side is completely turned away, we call it a new moon. There are also many phases when we can see part of the lit side of the Moon.

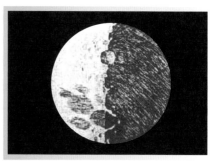

Galileo made these drawings of the phases of the Moon in 1610.

The Moon from Earth

Compare Galileo's drawings to these photos of the monthly phases of the Moon. How accurate were his drawings?

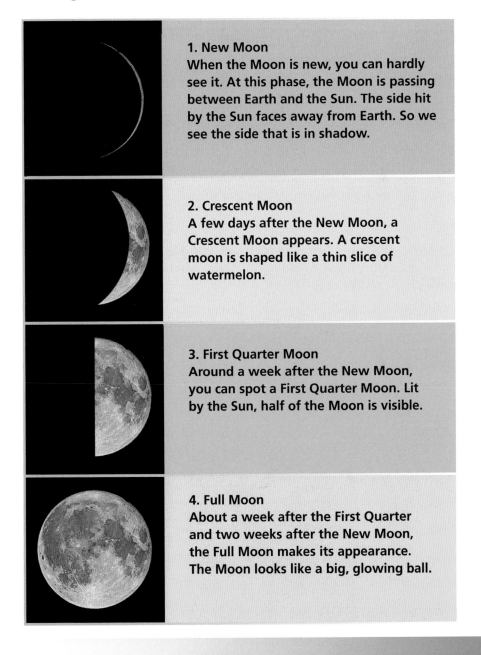

1. New Moon
When the Moon is new, you can hardly see it. At this phase, the Moon is passing between Earth and the Sun. The side hit by the Sun faces away from Earth. So we see the side that is in shadow.

2. Crescent Moon
A few days after the New Moon, a Crescent Moon appears. A crescent moon is shaped like a thin slice of watermelon.

3. First Quarter Moon
Around a week after the New Moon, you can spot a First Quarter Moon. Lit by the Sun, half of the Moon is visible.

4. Full Moon
About a week after the First Quarter and two weeks after the New Moon, the Full Moon makes its appearance. The Moon looks like a big, glowing ball.

The Moon and the Tides

Have you ever spent a day at the ocean? You may have noticed that the tide, or rise and fall of the water, changes throughout the day. Most places on Earth have two high tides and two low tides each day. Why?

The Moon is the main reason the tides change. Its gravity causes Earth's land, water, and atmosphere to bulge out toward the Moon. The water moves more easily than the land, so it bulges more. The water forms a tidal bulge, or big wave, which lags about an hour behind the movement of the Moon. In places where the water is bulging out, water levels rise, causing high tide. On other parts of Earth, water flows away, toward the bulge, causing low tide.

While the difference between high and low tide is only about two feet in the middle of the ocean, it can reach fifty feet at some places on the coast!

Close-up of Saturn's rings

Think about all you know about the solar system. You know that it is made up of the Sun and its satellites. You know that the Moon and other objects, such as meteors, comets, and asteroids, are part of the solar system too.

You are aware of the many changes that occur in your world, from the switch between day and night, to the seasons, to the phases of the Moon and the daily tides. You know that the movement of Earth through the solar system causes those changes. You've learned quite a bit. Galileo would be impressed!

Glossary

asteroid a rocky object that orbits the Sun in the asteroid belt and is less than one thousand kilometers across

axis the imaginary line on which Earth rotates, or spins

comet an object made of ice and dirt that travels around the Sun in a long orbit

Moon phase the shape of the lighted part of the Moon at a particular time

revolution one orbit

rotation one complete spin of an object on its axis

satellite an object that orbits another object

solar system the Sun and its satellites

space probe a spacecraft that gathers data without having any people on board

What did you learn?

1. How does the movement of Earth in space create cycles we all experience?

2. Why does the Moon seem to change in appearance as it goes through different phases each month?

3. Why is a year on Earth different from a year on Pluto?

4. **Writing** in Science The Sun's extreme heat and power cause actions to take place in the solar system. Write about the Sun's effects on the solar system. Include examples and details from the book to support your answer.

5. **Make Inferences** Other than Earth, the Moon is the only object in the solar system that has been visited by humans. Why do you think that is?

Genre	Comprehension Skill	Text Features	Science Content
Nonfiction	Make Inferences	• Diagrams • Captions • Maps • Glossary	Earth and Space

Scott Foresman Science 5.17

PEARSON

Scott Foresman

scottforesman.com

ISBN 0-328-13965-3

90000

9 780328 139651

Grouping Living Things

by Patricia Walsh

Vocabulary

class
classify
invertebrates
kingdom
phylum
species
vertebrate

Picture Credits

Every effort has been made to secure permission and provide appropriate credit for photographic material.
The publisher deeply regrets any omission and pledges to correct errors called to its attention in subsequent editions.

Photo locators denoted as follows: Top (T), Center (C), Bottom (B), Left (L), Right (R), Background (Bkgd).

Opener: Paul Nicklen/NGS Image Collection; 4 (T) ©Kennan Ward/Corbis;
5 (TCR, CAR, CAR1, CR, CBR, BCR) ©Darren Bennett/Animals Animals/Earth Scenes, (TL, CLA, CL) ©Darrell Gulin/Corbis;
6 (T) ©T. Beveridge/Visuals Unlimited, (CL) ©Stanley Flegler/Visuals Unlimited, (CL) Corbis, (CL) ©Michael Fogden/
Animals Animals/Earth Scenes, (BC) ©D. Robert & Lorri Franz/Corbis; 7 (T) ©Jerry Young/DK Images;
14 Paul Nicklen/NGS Image Collection; 19 (TL) ©American Museum of Natural History/DK Images;
22 Doug Wechsler /Nature Picture Library.

Unless otherwise acknowledged, all photographs are the copyright © of Dorling Kindersley, a division of Pearson.

ISBN: 0-328-13917-3